MW00886675

CLASS OF 2020

THIS NOTEBOOK BELONGS TO

Made in the USA
Coppell, TX
18 February 2020

15950875R00068